Advance Praise for *This small house, this big sky*

The range of Maria Rouphail's new book is delightful. What she invites into "her small house" of poetry is immense...everything under "this big sky." Whether invoking scenes from the ancient prophet Jeremiah to describe our environmental damage or humorously remembering her family's 1948 Ford, her free verse lines move with rhythmic life and imagery. Whether at dinner in a cafe in Philadelphia, "as tanks press toward Kyiv" or alone "lugging" her "petition up the root-snarled hill" to consult with trees, she takes us there.

—John Balaban, author of *Passing Through a Gate*

There is so much to cherish in Maria Rouphail's abundant, elegant *This small house, this big sky*, a volume with the scope and authority of ethnography and the warmth and amplitude of genealogy. Perhaps, more than anything, however, its most alluring element is the plaintive, full-throated, prayerful song of a poet willing to take profound risks and wield unforgettable language to metamorphose the daily into the heightened sweep of epic, even opera. With unflinching precision, Rouphail escorts us from the cupboards of the kitchen to the plenitude of the cosmos. This is a yearning, powerful book.

— Joseph Bathanti, North Carolina Poet Laureate (2012-14) & author of *Light at the Seam*

It's rare to finish reading a book of poetry moved to tears by its entirety. *This small house, this big sky* is that rare book. Maria Rouphail writes with a woman's sensibility—a daughter, mother, grandmother, and woman of faith—possessed by insistent memories and quaking fears for the future of civilization. Employing masterful command of poetic craft across a range of forms, Rouphail wrings beauty from each page: "mountains necklaced in cloud, / forests scarved with cobalt rivers, / a distant city gowned in lacteal air." ("Toronto Travel Notes"). But it is the naked depth of the poet's investment in her subjects which brought me to tears: "Listen to me lift my voice / on the street corner of my life" ("To My Mother and Father").

—Joan Barasovska, author of *Orange Tulips*

"Listen to me lift my voice," says Maria Rouphail at the start of her new collection, and these heartfelt poems merit our rapt attention. In language that shimmers and surprises, she converses with her beloved dead, seeking understanding and offering forgiveness, and also speaks of war, plague and what humans have done "beyond all mercy." Persona poems give voice to the Feminine, including women in the Bible, saints, mothers in Gaza and Syria, and our own Mother Earth "wounded unto death." Blazing through the darkness is the joy Rouphail finds in nature. With compassion, imagination, and skill, she beads her poems into a rosary for our broken world.

—Janis Harrington, author of *How to Cut a Woman in Half*

This small house, this big sky

by

Maria Rouphail

This small house, this big sky

Copyright © 2025 Maria Rouphail

All rights reserved. No part of this publication may be reproduced, distributed, or transmitted in any form or by any means, including photocopying, recording, or other electronic or mechanical methods, without the prior written permission of the publisher, except in the case of brief quotations embodied in critical reviews and certain other noncommercial uses permitted by copyright law. For permission requests, write to the publisher, addressed "Attention: Permissions Coordinator," at the address below.

This is a work of fiction. Unless otherwise indicated, all the names, characters, businesses, places, events and incidents in this book are either the product of the author's imagination or used in a fictitious manner. Any resemblance to actual persons, living or dead, or actual events is purely coincidental.

ISBN: 978-1-959346-84-5 (Paperback)

Library of Congress Control Number: 2024952890

Cover Design: Erin Mann
Book Design: Erin Mann
Cover Artwork: Paul Rouphail

Printed in the United States of America.

First printing 2025.

Redhawk Publications
The Catawba Valley Community College Press
2550 Hwy 70 SE
Hickory NC 28602
https://redhawkpublications.com

*for my beloved family,
living and dead*

and for my friends

*and in loving memory of
Rafik Michel Raphael (1937-2024)*

Also by Maria Rouphail:

Apertures (Finishing Line Press, 2013)
New Women's Voices finalist

Second Skin (Main Street Rag Press, 2015)

All the Way to China (Finishing Line Press, 2022)
Finalist in both the University of Wisconsin Brittingham Poetry and the Blue Light Press competitions.

Contents

To My Mother and Father — 15

I.

This small house, this big sky — 18
Diagnosis — 19
Mother — 20
The Origin of Poetry — 21
What a Friend said to my Face one Afternoon — 22
September — 24
Five Women — 25
Mary Magdalene Theorizes — 30
Seeing my Mother from the Pulpit of a Church — 32
Samaria — 34

II.

On Seeing a Celebrated Author in the Newspaper — 37
I go Ask the Trees — 39
The Poetry Workshop: Storm Damage — 40
The Poetry Workshop: Comment by a Participant — 41
Maker of Metaphors — 42
To My Second Grade Teacher — 44
On a Renowned Poet I Admire — 45
I Buried a Little Bird Today — 46
Pandemic, 1918 — 47
Digressions on a '48 Ford — 49

As Tanks Press Toward Kyiv	50
To Jeremiah, Who Mourned the Calamitous Earth	52
Uncle Sam Offers a Prayerful Apology	54
Still Life	55
Grandfathers: Two Photographs	57
Toronto Travel Notes	61
This Weird and Frantic Dream I Had	65
To a Mother in Gaza	67

III.

Journal Entry	71
In the Penumbra of Adolescence	72
Appalachian Morning	74
What the Venerable Bede Told	75
O, Doves!	77
Stephansplatz	78
House Painter, New Jersey	79
Light as Seen from a Bedside	80
The Bus	81
Abuela	82
Aftershock	83
En alta mar	84
Sea Poem	86
Things that Lift my Heart and Make it Glad	87
Horses	89
In the Groove, Painting in Plein-Air	90
Crater of Popocatépetl	91
Variations on a Theme of a Tenement	93

IV.

Air Traffic Control, London to Mauritius	99
Flashback on a Morning Walk in Early Spring	101
Imagining Wanda	102
Appliance Repairman	104
Asher	106
Iowa Scenes	107

V.

Meeting for the First Time	113
A Young Child Speaks of a Tornado	114
After the Storm	115
The Plague Ship	116
What I Can Say	117
Ekphrasis on an Icon of the Theotokos	118
Prayer in a Dark Season	119
The Bread Maker's Last Testament	120
Resurrection in *Nueba Yol*	121
Notes	124
Acknowledgments	127
About the Author	130

*In a murderous time / the heart breaks and breaks
and lives by breaking. / It is necessary to go
into dark and deeper dark / and not to break.*

Stanley Kunitz, "The Testing Tree"

*Existence can't be so poor a thing / as living . . . inside a body /
only to become mere stubble and ash.*

Óscar Hahn, "Muerte de mi Madre"

To My Mother and Father

If I am lucky,
God will give me
twenty years
before I meet you
wherever you now glory.
From this day on,
I will work to be the self
I am not yet,
holy and brave
with an open heart and hand,
just as you tried to make me.
Two decades isn't so much to ask.
Listen to me lift my voice
on the street corner of my life
to make good of failure, fire, loss,
of roads taken or not,
that brought me to this place.

I.

My mother comes to me in a dream. She asks me to tell her what I long for, and I begin to pour out my heart. She listens with the most loving attention. "Embrace what is small, what is vulnerable," she says. But just as I am about to ask what she means by her words, the dream ends. I wake up.

                                              Journal entry

This small house, this big sky

> *Shapes of things: so much the same*
> *they feel like eternal forms*
> (Adrienne Rich, "Sources")

This small house
my heart's center
where the world entered and sat down
and I greeted it
as a mysterious guest
my first words swelling into
sentences and song
north to the barred owl in the backyard oak
and the clothesline strung with bedsheets post to post
south to the sawmill
and the draft horses pulling flatbeds of logs
east where a gravel road snaked toward the bay
and long clouds steamed from the loud freight train
west and a highway curving into the pines
and the pond where we swam
where a laughing boy in my class
did not drown one afternoon
but caught polio instead
he never walked again
his mother cried
my mother kept me close
and the sky stared at us in silence
every day in those days
I wondered why
that boy
and not me.

Diagnosis

Still marking the day,
fifty-four years.
Still counting
vials, syringes,
Roentgens of cobalt-60 burning
too late, too late.

A clear spring morning.
The doctor entered the examining room,
your open medical file in hand,
and words that seared.

So, it was *that*, Mama, which stalked you
down the generations.
Now it gripped you hard in the middle of your life.
You had (the doctor said) only so much time.

This thing passed down,
woman to woman
like a quilt.
How young I was,
stark faced,
flayed by sandstorm thoughts
your tongue did not have to speak.

They burn even now, long after
pregnancies and babies at the breast—
Did I give you a body like mine?
Poor daughter!
It, too, will make orphans.

Mother

Looking back,
there were signs.
Unheard-of malaise,
fevers bedding you for days
and glazed eyes jaundiced
in their watery sockets.

As though upthrust from earth's core,
archipelagoes of swollen organs
hardened under your skin—
spleen, liver, gut.
Lymph nodes the size of acorns
clustered in neck and groin.

For months I watched
your body delete the codes
of its various functional parts—
breast, lung, liver, bone.
You were a planet imploding
in the cosmic cold.

That day,
when your life sank forever into a dark
hulk of dismantled flesh,
was the coldest, though it wasn't winter.
And I, a stalk of ice-riven switchgrass,
tossed and whipped in a glacial wind.

The Origin of Poetry

I'm sorry said the notes I penciled my mother
to make her look at me, coax her to forgive
whatever I'd done to put her in a mood.

I was seven or eight and learning cursive.
I wrote left-handed, *I will be good.*
I'd leave my words where I knew she'd find them,
folded against the saltshaker on the counter beside the stove.

She'd hug me, of course, and tell me not to worry.
But before too long, the darkness filled her again.
It made her eyes drift away like little sailboats
disappearing into the mouth of a river at dusk.
She didn't see me waving at her to come back.

Mama, it will be alright.
My mother died before I learned the full story.
I kept on, putting our grief to paper
as though I were draining a wound
to save both of our lives.

But it's okay now. I grew up. And I still write her.
Thank you, Mama. I owe you everything.

**What a friend said to my face one afternoon,
at my own kitchen table**

>   *(with a line from Lynn Emanuel)*

Should've been you.
She turned a butter knife between thumb and forefinger,
laid it down, then sipped her coffee—

You're the one with the messed-up genes, after all.
From my dead mother, true, who got them from hers.
No doubt those ill-fated ladies gifted them to me.
Only a matter of time, I half-joked—

Should've been you, been thinking that for a while now—
Said this in her assassin's voice
she used mostly for stories about her boss.
So, how was I such a beacon of health?
While she, with a child and a clean family history,
succumbed to the scalpel that sliced
her woman-self away. Said all this
while pointing to the flat balloon of her blouse.

Wasn't supposed to happen to me—
She was just past forty, parents still alive.
Showed me an old photo where she's
dancing with friends.
Party Girl. That was her nickname, she said,
her voice trailing off.
How she must have missed those days!
Who wouldn't want them back?

Or the young body so perfect in red.
She was playing with the knife again.
So, what do you know of fear?

She cut her gaze at me.
Enough, I said
and raised the flat of my hand
against the blade of her curse.
Enough, that when
she got up and left, I locked the door
while the blood in me rose high,
sloshing in my skull that whole afternoon
like a lake behind a dam.

September

has the smell of my mother dying.
Her cancer breath. A fetid rasp.
I watched the woman-flesh that birthed
my sister and me unravel into ash and earth.

Only weeks before
she'd had a birthday, and we had a cake.
It was August, the month of Leo's heat.
Then, September brought my mother
her *forever* day.
Her day of *never again*.

How to explain things,
except to say I always felt fated.
Since I was a September child,
some fall season would surely mark my end.

Years passed. Then, many years.
But the unequal sun of October brought
not death, but life. New lives, in fact.
November, too, despite its lengthening nights.
Children. A grandchild. Lights in the darkness.
Mama, you can see them, can't you?
All this copper and gold,
these diamond trees shining in the silver of late fall?

Five Women

I.

Mary of Nazareth

Light! How I loved
to watch it creep down the folds

of the mountains, the way it
pooled in the olive trees and scissored

through fat lobes of summer cloud.
How it tossed and turned on the lake

before a storm. And then it entered me
moving like fire, and within it a voice.

Not flattery, but fright made me stand stock
still and listen to a greeting

and an invitation. What words
were these to someone like me?

Yet, schooled in wonder, my heart said, *Yes.*
Which is when a seed took root,

and for nine months flourished.
Blood of my blood, bone of my bone.

I didn't tell my husband-to-be,
God's very Self is growing here—

The man who loved my boy and me
learned all that in a dream.

II.

Martha of Bethany

They say I fussed too much,
that I was insistent. Bossy, even.
A model of pointless worry.

I'm on record as resenting my sister's dreaminess,
the way she sat at our friend's feet,
hanging on his every word

when she ought to have been helping me.
Sure, I told her off—after all,
we had an honored guest

and a house-full of his companions to feed.
Who would help me get the meal ready?
Light the Shabbat candles?

I'd been cooking all day. But when he
said *Let her be*, as though she had
as much right as any man

at the table, I sat myself down.
Like my sister.
I, too, burned with dreams.

III.

The Canaanite Woman

I was a despised foreigner,
and his countrymen pushed me away.

But with my daughter so sick,
how could I not persist?

How could I let this man pass by
without tendering my plea?

You'd be right to think I was fired up
when I put the case for my tormented child,

her ravings, her foaming mouth. A wild
demon's work, some busybodies said.

At first I thought he hadn't heard, for all
the noise his friends made to shut me up.

But I kept on, until he had to turn and face me.
Sir! I cried out. *Will you help me—*

I'm not sure he entirely believed
the words he gave me in reply,

reminding me of the mission to his own people,
and my tribe's difference.

But I gathered myself for my child's sake—
Even dogs eat the scraps from their master's table.

Then, as I fell silent, his face changed.
I will do as you ask, he said.

That night, as I rocked her,
my little girl dreamed deeply in my arms.

IV.

The Samaritan Woman

Could this old well speak,
had it a living tongue,
what gossip would it tell
of stillborn babies and straying husbands,
trysts made, betrothals broken.
No stranger ever spoke to a woman here,
unless he was up to no good.
I cared less about others' opinions
than for this well, as deep as my dreams.
Covered in sweat and dust
he wasn't what anyone expected—
a road-weary man asking me
for a drink from the well.
Of course, I served him.
What decent person would let another
faint with thirst?
Now let me set the story straight,
lest you believe the gossip about
my supposed notorious past.
You'd have to know the ancients,
their penchant for poetry.
We talked about husbands,
just not the fleshy kind.
When I felt his kindness,
I ran and told the people.
The good news spread like fire
over the land.

V.

Mary of Magdala

Who would believe what I had seen?
Not the men who followed him.
It took time and a woman.

Most of them fled, their hearts crushed
by the sight of his flayed body,
its bloodied nakedness.

But we women stayed
through the dying of that day,
so he wouldn't be alone in his torment.

In the morning, with dawn seeping
over the hilltops, I went
back and found the tomb empty.

That's when I heard a voice
in the cool blue-violet light—
Mary.

He commissioned me to tell the others.
I ran to where they hid and said,
I have seen him.

A fire rose in me,
as I proclaimed that good news
on the first day of the week.

Mary Magdalene Theorizes

He said *Don't*
when I reached to touch him.
I didn't quite get it, but I didn't press him, either.
I had to remember
I wasn't his mother or aunt,
his wife, sister, or somebody's mother-in-law.
I wasn't a man, like the ones
who followed him around for three years.
Perhaps the holes in his body still hurt.
His skin might have been hot and tight from the light
that blasted away the stone.
He might have been, somehow, wet
and sticky from the afterbirth of his new body.
Hadn't he been a corpse for nearly three days?
Now he was clean, gleaming.
It was five in the morning, the sky was black and purple,
the sun was just breaking over the hilltops.
I had been weeping for hours.
Imagine the shock when I heard someone call my name!
Of course, I wanted to touch him.
Maybe I strode right up to his face, and he didn't object.
Or maybe he didn't say anything.
Maybe the story changed, after I told it,
and I was made to fail at knowing the difference
between daring and propriety, fear and faith.
I was clingy and possessive, it was said for too long,
the way a woman supposedly is in these situations.
Lot's wife, for example.

She was that way, they say, mourning the walls
where her children left their handprints,
her lovely loom.
She couldn't move on, and now
that's what they say about me.
How do they know I didn't simply love him,
was amazed he was alive.
My whole self, ringing like a bell.

Seeing my mother from the pulpit of a church I don't belong to

> *i pleaded with her, what could i do,*
> *oh what could i have done?*
>
> (Lucille Clifton)

In the dream,
I am invited in
and I enter.

I am asked to speak
and I speak
about women, their voicelessness
in a church that in its first days spoke
to the hearts of the enslaved and the violated.
Where the barren and the betrayed,
castaways and the condemned,
found food, a clean room.
And their hearts dilated with the heat of divinity.

I finish saying these words,
and a hundred hands reach from the pews
and rest on my head.

They lower a white chasuble over my shoulders,
a white stole around my neck.
They give a shepherd's crook into my right hand
No, no, I say. *Not me, I'm not the one—*

And then I see her
at the wheel of the black De Soto coupe,
just outside, in front of this church

I don't belong to.

It's raining hard,
but I can make her out from the sidewalk.
I hear her say, *C'mon, let's go.*
I scramble to find my things,
if I can remember where I left them—
umbrella, purse, the stuff of ordinary life—
it's what always happens when she shows up like this.
Maybe she'll take me with her this time, I think.

I run outside to the curb. *Mama!*
But there is only the boulevard dividing here from there.
And the rain, the rain.

Samaria

    (after Muriel Rukeyser)

I am the city
You want to enter

In this valley
shivering with light

I am listening
For your feet

All my windows and towers
are open

to the striding wind
and to the trees shaking in the wind-wake

of your voice
that asked for water

How thirsty you were
that day by the well

II.

*Even the trees don't know
he name of this storm.*

On Seeing a Celebrated Author in the Newspaper

A blank and sluggish day
Indecisive as a stalled weather front

I tell myself: Start writing, start anywhere—
Keep going until lightning flares and cool rains fall

Begin with the black-clad woman looking out
From page fourteen of the book section
                    in the Sunday *Times*

The photo of her accomplished neck, rings of creamy flesh
The clavicular strings and taut manubrial attachments

Chin glowing in light filtered through sheer curtains
The way the facial ligatures hold

Her head just so for the camera
The sweep of her hair, a silver cirrus

Between arched eyebrows and light irises
Corrugations of skin suggesting habitual thought

And the mouth pursed in a high-gloss
Smile of triumph, as if to say

I have lived to write this magnificent tale
I have prevailed

It's the face I imagine she's given
The heroine of her much lauded novel

About a woman who loved a man
And was rewarded with betrayal

Or maybe he died in a war. Perhaps
There wasn't a man at all   Or even a war

This face on the page—it's as old as mine
More beautiful, I'd have to say

But the brain behind it, encased in flawless bone
No more word-obsessed, filled with story.

I go and ask the trees

before the winter storm arrives,
to please stay on their feet.

It makes no difference,
hurricane or blizzard—

in a crowd of hardwoods,
a gale is a gale,

and rain when turned to ice
will lop a stalwart trunk

and crush a roof's stout hip
sure as any blow, bone on bone.

This rite of mine before a storm,
lugging my petition up the root-snarled hill

to the beeches and oaks where they huddle
like old horses—

I watch their crowns toss and thrash,
I stroke their lichen-dappled skin with the flats of my hands.

Steady, I whisper.

But I can hear them lurch and creak
in the surge and stagger of the goading wind.

The Poetry Workshop: Storm Damage

Your sister wonders why you still comb
the rubble of your mother's storms.
Why you've not yet fork-lifted to the side of the road
all the mildewed plywood and pulverized glass from your
I'm-too-old-for-this-shit self.
Why, like a perpetual refugee, you still pick through
wisps of clothing and paper, long after each gale closed its
gray eye and drifted out to sea.
Cyclones come and go, your sister says.

But you wonder how her own roof and door stood fast
against such muscled winds as ripped pines by their
splayed roots from the side of the hill.
Even now they lie, tangled hanks from the scalp
of the earth weeping red clay.

"Look at the new trees," your sister says,
"How tall they've grown after all these years in the sun."
You want to tidy up your yard, too. But you can't help it.
You're always listening, waiting, scanning the sky
for scud clouds, rising wind.

The Poetry Workshop: Comment by a Participant

*The middle-aged lady read her lines, and people snickered.
First time in a workshop, and there she stood—
poem in her trembling hand, like in a dream
where you're walking without a stitch down a city street.
Everybody's gawking or looking quickly away.
Not a damn thing you can do but press on.
The poet waited for a smirking woman—
a pimple-faced blonde with cat's-eye spectacles—
to regain her composure.
The blonde pursed her lips and turned to stare out a window.
What to do with these self-important* cognoscenti*?
Still, the poet thought she should explain herself:
"So, critique-wise," she stammered, "what I'm attempting
to show is the lingering aftermath of a parent's
depression—in an adult child—the debris field—"
Always a bad move, surrendering to marauders the keys
to a locked door. After all, the poem is pure metaphor.
Her naked thoughts' clothing. The poem's tidy raiment.
And what was not clean, pressed and discreetly accessorized?
What dishevelment in scud clouds, hills that weep wet clay?*

Maker of Metaphors
(or, There were trees behind her house
and an RCA Victor in the living room)

1 Tenor

Not quite a forest,
but woods dense enough,
northwest from the back fence
all the way to Route 9, two miles.

A pine-coned trail from the swing set
wide enough for kindergarten feet to
wade deeper into dappled darkness
What is this smell she loves,
the rain-damp forest smell?
On the path, a light-gilt clearing and
a small tulip tree, leaves splashed
with sun and wind.

2 Vehicle

In the living room,
a television set,
first in her family.
Black-and-white.
Weeknights,
she roosts with

> her parents on the sofa,
> fixed on the new-fangled
> spectacle beamed to the working
> classes of the newly post-war.
> Her father leans forward.
> *Who is he pointing to on the screen?*
> Somebody famous about to
> wow the live studio audience.
> The camera now pans
> to a hundred clapping hands—

3 Object(s) Transformed

In the waft of pine and petrichor,
the little tulip tree lifts its arms.
How loud its leaf-hands are as they clap,
        she says to herself.
The tall trees, too—how they
clap in delirious applause.
How these woods are peopled
with trees nodding to one another,
murmuring about something just out of sight,
wheeling on the haunch of the wind.

This burst and flare of the *as if* power.
She laughs at the trick of her mind's eye.
She will play it again and again
As she learns to make pictures with words.

To My Second Grade Teacher, Mrs. Althea Kirk

I was the dark-skinned girl with a foreign name
who'd never seen mountains.
But when you played the upright piano
and we sang, *My Country, 'Tis of Thee*,
I dreamed of them.

Didn't you teach us to dream?
That boy with a stutter, red-faced with sobbing.
How you soothed him.
As I fidgeted and chatted with my neighbor,
you didn't scold, but bent low, and in
your quiet voice asked if I'd help you
with the afternoon reading.
I want to remember saying, *Yes, Ma'am*.
Most likely I only nodded, looking down at my shoes
with a seven-year-old's wordless shame.

When the hour arrived, and we pulled
three chairs into a little triangle,
you called to a girl with a lisp,
and the boy with the stutter,
putting them in my charge.
They took turns reading aloud
as I carefully listened,
gently sounding out the words,
only if they needed, just as you did every day.

Which is how I learned for the first time
what was mine to give, if I could shape it—
a patient ear like yours,
a voice I did not need to swallow,
a tongue that helped another to say
thee   sing   pride

On a Renowned Poet I Admire
          (Berlin, 2016)

He achieved greatness in his day,
winning the world's crown.

He celebrated the delights of the body,
but was never crude or brutish. For him,

to be enfleshed was to membered in the Whole,
which is to say, Beauty itself.

He knew, too, that the touch of the mortal Other
made him human. Thus on the page, the fragmentary

female: breast and lip, the kohl-rimmed eye,
but only in celebration of mutual love.

Here, the synecdoche of Muse and Spouse
in the commingling of bodies—

an old-fashioned, outmoded trope
at whose stirrings he made his art.

Looking back at his life, he claimed
never to have sung in praise of nothing.

His words must be true, since for him
the incarnate was everything,

and he, as well he knew,
was only a poet.

I Buried a Little Bird Today

in the backyard
behind the old beech.
What sort of bird I cannot say,
or its age or where in its body
it suffered the fatal flaw.
I only held in one hand
its beating wings, the closed claw
and gaping beak,
its shuddering feathered head.
And when it stopped, I dug a hole
and to the beech I said,
Be kind, be kind.

Pandemic, 1918

for MR, who lived and died in another century

1.

Wind-waft and a brown leaf
lofted from a forest floor.
Bone-scrabble of dry dirt—
a forewarning,

        and the story
two generations told again and again
about the microbes' fatal power, and the grief
of the young mother whose sibylline brain
showed her what lay ahead—

        Old Scratch
wrapped in black serge (they said)
stalking the forest (of her fear).
And the field at the forest's edge
where she went walking (on a bright fall day)
with her perfect infant daughter.
He swooped out of the dark trees,
nor'easter-like, snatching the baby from her arms.
(she had no way to stop him).
Then he and the child disappeared
into the forest.

What could she do
on that hot tenement night,
but bolt upright in bed,
nudge her snoring husband awake.

2.

He said *sweet jeezuz*
He said *what are you caterwauling about*
He said *you know how I need to get up early*
He said *you had a bad dream for crissake that's all*
He said *you probably ate somethin' that disagreed with you*
He said *you know how you get when you're pregnant*
He said *you always make such a goddam big deal outta nothin'*
He said *you gotta to go back to sleep and leave me in peace*
He said *you better stop crying,*
or I'm gonna give you somethin' real to cry about

3.

So I did /for my daughter's sake / My second, pure light / I conceived her when I was only five months past birthing her sister / I woke up in a friendless hour of night / to tell her father the fright I had / But I tamped it all down / The panic and the panting / Swallowed it / for her and for me / She churned and churned a long time/ as though she heard thunder crack / Waves of her father's voice pounding into her embryo ears / through all the layers of my skin and muscle meant to keep her safe/ I felt her foot push against my ribs / like she wanted to run away / So I rubbed it and I whispered / *It's alright It's alright* / Sure, it was a stormy summer night when the dream came / Before the Fever stole her / Stole so many babies in that year.

Digressions on a '48 Ford

Not navy, but the cool blue of a bay in astronomical
twilight. My father's first car. Bought it used, five years
after the War. He was forty. Moved us from the south
Bronx to south Jersey where he'd found a job mixing
cocktails instead of boilermakers.

Our blue Ford! The luminous planets of its hubcaps,
its chrome-ringed headlamps. And the tufted upholstery—
such drawing-room swank in dove-gray. *Flying Goose*,
Mama called it, after the flexed-for-flight bird silvered in
mid-honk on the hood.

In the first days, my father battled the gears. He soon
forged a smooth alliance of choke, clutch, and brake. When
he tried to teach Mama to drive, she, too, stripped the
gears and flooded the engine. The Flying Goose snorted
and bucked, more mule than sleek bird, plunging my little
sister and me in our winter coats from the back seat to the floor.

But enough about the car. Except to add, there were no
safety belts, airbags, or kiddie seats in those days. When at
breakfast on a Thursday morning Mama announced her
plan to drive all the way to Philly, I watched my father
lower his coffee cup to look at her.

Next day, after she'd rouged her cheeks in the living
room mirror, smoothed a stray lock behind her ear, she
headed out the front door, car key in hand and us in tow.
I turned to see Papa huffing down the front steps, following us.
Oh, no! I heard him breathe, *Not with my baby
girls! No, not with them—*

As Tanks Press Toward Kyiv
(and you gather with family in a restaurant in Philadelphia)

You want to know why it persists,
this curse of the human,
pyromania at the heart's core,
the dream and drive to master the Other
as we torment the earth into acid and ash.

Even now,
six time zones east of where you sit
gathered with family at a restaurant in Philadelphia,
missiles explode over towns in Ukraine.

At table, beside a large window in this Queen Village café,
you side-glance at pedestrians trundling in hooded
coats along the icy sidewalk, tacking into the winter wind.

How to explain it,
but they cause you to remember your mother-in-law.
She comes into focus, a luminous streak out of infinite darkness—

Her words, in a restaurant much like this one,
translated from the Arabic by her eldest son,
about the streets in Cairo where they all lived in those days,
especially in front of their apartment building—
a rent in the pavement deep and wide.
If she tripped into it, she quipped,
no one would ever find her.
Hyperbole, no doubt.

But to your ear, words
a frightened child might whisper—your own words
during a shopping trip to Gimbels, when you and your
mother were separated among racks of winter coats.

You were only three, but old enough
for the shock of clarity that comes before grief,
old enough for your brain to form the silent words,
I am lost—
Then you began to wail.

At this moment,
six hours east,
fire rains down
on houses and hospitals,
on fathers and mothers and babies,
just as in Aleppo and Baghdad.

Need you say it?
These living and dead
are no different than your own.
The earth is no less a wonder
than on the first days of its birth,
but how old now, and wounded unto death.

And you want to scream at God, *We are lost!*
Why did you give us the craving for fire?
Why the hypnotic allure of flames?
Why a holocaust, O Lord, always a holocaust?

To Jeremiah, Who Mourned the Calamitous Earth

"They covered their heads . . . because of the stricken soil."
                              Jeremiah 14: 3-4

You knew nothing
of spinning planets,
the ocean's cyclical fevers,
meanders of the trade winds,
the oscillating weight of the atmosphere.

What you did see
was plain enough,
and ground-level grim—
day after day
a vacant blue dome,
pustules of cloud
on a windless horizon.

You saw a river silt up,
a lakebed crack like a plate.
You saw grape vines shrivel,
and wheat droop on the stalk.
Your heart broke with sobs
when a doe fled her nursling
and a donkey stretched his futile tongue
for a wisp of airborne wet.

As the land tossed in its fitful dream of water,
only the olive trees withstood,
and the snakes.

If today you could see, from the black heights of space,
rivers of smoke twisting in the stratosphere,
storms the size of mountain ranges,
calving glaciers, bleached coral, corpses of sea turtles,
felled forests in Amazonia and Canada's fire-gutted floors,

and if you said El Niño, hydrocarbons,
Kelvin waves, extinctions, atmospheric oceans—
words from a realm other than the poetics of prophecy,
your lament would be no less anguished.

We know too well
what we have done with the gift we were given,
and what we have failed to do.
The proof is clear, you'd say,
about our hungers and murderous rages.

What grieving god wouldn't hold back the rains,
or unleash them, striking the soil
from which our food and flesh come?

**Repenting of His Wrongdoing,
Uncle Sam Offers a Prayerful Apology
to Nuestra Señora de Guadalupe**

Tonantzin earthmother,
princess clothed with the sun and stars,
look upon me.

Lady whose feet crushed the Serpent,
let me see your face.

Aztec queen ravished by pale-skin *invasores*
who drove their king's flag into your body
in the name of the Father
and of the Son and of the Holy Ghost,
I stand before you.

And, wind-borne lady,
peasant girl with iron-black hair,
colonized by *explotadores*,
do not despise me,

though I deserve to be despised.

Santísima farm worker, harvester of vegetables and fruit,
Inmaculada cleaner of hotel rooms and airport toilets,
show me how to change my *conquistador* heart,
I implore you,

for even I have some regard for your name.

¡*Virgencita y madrecita!*

I took your little children
and locked them in cages
at the border of my fire-driven country.

Guadalupe,
forgive me the unforgivable.

Still Life

> (after William Michael Harnett,
> *The Old Cupboard Door*, a painting)

You lift it gently from the highest
shelf of the closet, loosen it from the tight
wedge of your stowed purses and scarves,
this six-by-four-inch jewelry box,
reliquary of an earlier life.
Carry it to the dresser. Open it
and lay the pieces one by one
before the icon of the Theotokos—

a broken rosary,
your mother's wedding band,
two stray pearls,
a papier mâché fish slathered in bright
turquoise and green acrylic paint
your younger son made in preschool,
two plastic heart-shaped pins that say,

> "I ♡ Robert" and "I ♡ Paul"—

your little boys, side-by-side
on your lapel at every teachers' meeting,

and the poem about a bird with broken wings
your mother penciled on lined paper,
smoke-deckled and water-stained
from the apartment fire
your husband and you survived.

She'd written the poem for her brother,
your uncle who was a figure painter.

A father, too, of more children
than the only son you knew as your first cousin.

No one ever figured out how many others there were,
or if they lived, or if their mothers grieved
their children's absent father,

or even it was for them
he heaved his riven life
over the balcony of a building in Manhattan.
It was 1964.

You finger the broken rosary.
Your uncle gifted it to your mother.
From Germany. Or, maybe Mexico.
It was certainly after the War,
but before he decided
that everything he had done
was beyond all mercy—
Our Father, Hail Mary, Glory Be—

You know it now.
You know his sister's prayers
were never enough to save him.

Grandfathers: Two Photographs

*"I want you to know the worst and be free from it.
I want you to know the worst and still find good"*

(John Balaban, "Words for My Daughter")

I.

Here are the grandfathers
in black and white.
Abuelo, grand-père,
fathers of children
begotten and abandoned,
mothers crushed.
Though strangers in life,
they could have been twin brothers
in their perfection of cruelty.

They became something like in-laws,
on the day before Hiroshima,
when their offspring married
in the parish church
of St Pius in the Bronx.

See them now, long after their deaths,
posed side-by-side on their
granddaughter's writing desk,
each man coffined in his own six-by-four
dollar-store metal and glass frame.

II.

Here is Herbert, Quebec City-born, father of the girl
who became the bride.
See him, centered in a group of infantry
of the New York National Guard.
Someone has written in white ink:
"Company 4, 71st Division, Pine Camp."
Herbert poses in the center, flanked by two soldiers
who like him hold their mess kits,
a perfect trinity of broad shoulders and flat bellies.
Herbert had a taste for hooch,
the drinking and selling of it.
Drove bootleg over the border,
New York to Quebec and back,
for almost fifteen years.

III.

Clean-shaven Herbert, so young and fit,
your lips parted in a sly smile,
how irresistible you are in your service hat and puttees—
no wonder girls fell for you.
And in your wife-beater, too—such irony!—
enhancing the muscular arms that powered
your fists against your wife's skull again and again.
You caused the fine tissues of her eyes
to turn purple. You pulled hanks
of her hair from their roots. You bloodied her mouth.
She made her body into a shield against your roaring angers.
Then you tried to silence her forever, tightening
a plumber's chain around her neck.
Only Margie, your oldest, shrieking and weeping
as she held a knife to your throat, broke your grip.

Herbert, in this photo everyone is older than you,
and weary from what wars?

IV.

Here is "Sinapo," nicknamed by Key West Conchs
for pronouncing red "snapper" in his forever-broken English.
In the faded photo, he is a bloated man in his dotage.
But in the stories of his youth, a dashing seducer.
Gambler. Party boy. No cigar-making for him.
Good for a laugh and bottles of Cuban rum
when he slithered into the world
of teenaged Clara Gallo in Guanabacoa.
No one ever told how Sinapo managed to woo her.
She left her family's home for a new life in Key West.
He promptly filled her with a baby boy, and then another
and then he simply disappeared.

V.

Padre—*only in terms of biology.*
Abuelo—*from the Arabic: father, man of wisdom—*
only by the conventions of language.

Sinapo, you knew the girl was dying.
Yet you abandoned her with a toddler and an infant on the way.
Clara, barely out of her teens, rescued by her mother and sister,
returned to Cuba where she birthed
your younger son, Roberto. Then she died.

On the baby's baptismal record,
en la parroquia de Nuestra Señora de la Asunción,
someone wrote, Victoria Gallo, madrina *and* soltera,
Clara's younger and unmarried sister who raised your little boy
until he was old enough to go searching for you

in Key West, Tampa, and New York City.
He found you, a grizzled man
with several women and many children.
You had abandoned them, too.

Roberto was drafted into the US Army.
And then he met Herbert's Margie (the girl who
saved her mother from death),
married her on August 5, the day before a B-29
dropped the A-bomb on Hiroshima.

VI.

Grandfathers, *abuelo* and *grand-père,*
who danced at no child's birth, baptism, or wedding,
who gave no daughters away in marriage,
who blessed no sons or daughters on their firstborn
or had anyone named in your honor,
did you know your children tried to love you?

Now their daughter, herself grown old,
wants to believe you gave some sign of sorrow
before your bodies unspooled toward death,
wants to believe that somewhere in their hereafter,
your children have forgiven you.

In memory of them,
your granddaughter forgives you.

Toronto Travel Notes

I.

Carolina to Canada

Flight 8835

Waking from the cocoon of night,
Earth puts on its day clothes—

mountains necklaced in cloud,
forests scarved with cobalt rivers,
a distant city gowned in lacteal air.

We are mostly quiet, content in our laptops or books,
though a tiny infant reminds us
of our animal hungers.

The seatbelt sign blinks off and the cabin crew
push the refreshment trolley up the aisle,
offering sodas, juice, and hot drinks.

The sun, too, ties on its yellow apron,
reaches through the starboard windows
and serves us strong light with our morning coffee.

II.

Nahkt the Weaver
at the Royal Ontario Museum, Queen's Park

How lightly he lies on the display case floor,
this young man from Thebes.
No more than twenty, the museum note says,
when something—disease or accident—took him
too soon from the loom he worked each day.

How carefully they prepared him,
his grieving mother and father,
for his encounter with the gods.
Their frail son's slender arched feet,
narrow shoulders, and his perfect skull,
broken for burial. Ribs, too.
For the brain, heart, and liver must be extracted,
if his spirit were to voyage into paradise.
They lie beside his body now, like little stones.

How fine the linen mantle draping his supine frame,
collar bone to ankles, no doubt like cloth he wove in the family
workshop, pride of parents who knew their son's worth.

What would they say about their boy's bones in this place?
Yet here am I, three millennia later,
stopping to behold Nahkt the Weaver,
paying my respects,
writing this poem in his praise.

III.

Abdulrazak Gurnah could write a story about these digs,
I say to myself, as we pass Club Zanzibar on Yonge Street

A friend wants me to know this place
is a city landmark, a big deal
especially in the early days—
adult club, juke joint, barrel house.
It looks like a post-pandemic jerry rig,
though it's been here since the fifties.
The friend says the beefy guys
hunched over cigarettes at the entrance
are harmless.

Maybe. But I'm thinking Gurnah, his novels
and the 60's war that drove him from his ancestral island—
I mean the actual place,

Zanzibar. Perennial apple of imperial eyes.
More than cloves were traded in squalid stalls.
Much more than ivory was trafficked across a gulf.

IV.

**Departure
after a light lunch on Carlton Street**

Too brief, too brief, this reunion with old friends,
reminiscences, gossip, complaints of life-long
labor and age.
Immigrants all, what kin remain in the old country?
Who has left for good?
Whose children have children, there and here?
Who is now grayer, fatter, diabetic, or dead?

And the barbarities of wealth—
Who let the rich seize the horizon for themselves alone,
their glassy high-rise palaces erasing sky and shore?
Where is the view of Lake Ontario in ordinary windows?

This weird and frantic dream I had

about a young man with a rare and fatal disease.
Doctors say it's necessary to store his
blood in a tusk. (Ivory? Horn?)
The young man's father, in an effort to
help his son, stations himself on a subway platform in a
major metropolis at rush hour (New York? Chicago?)
The elder man, an accomplished pianist,
places the tusk and a collection basket at the
feet of a baby grand on which he plays a brilliant
Prokofiev to the echoing, indeed thundering,
applause of commuters, overwhelming
the underground din.
The son stands nearby as people toss coins into the basket.
Some hug him or clap a sympathetic hand on his shoulder.
A TV crew arrives. To their (inaudible) questions,
the young man utters the words
"despair," "disgust," "dismay"—it's difficult to hear.
But the father hears. And he rises up in a rage,
overturning the piano bench, slamming the keyboard shut.
He kicks the tusk with his son's blood
and the basket of cash onto the tracks.
The reporters and onlookers gasp
just as the train I need to take roars in, blowing past my stop.
Sweetjeezuz! Now I'm running—

At which point I startle awake with the clock radio
pouring the news into my ears:
A freight train two-miles long and carrying industrial chemicals
has derailed in Ohio, spilling all of its poisons and exploding
in a fireball over a small city.
A mass shooter in Colorado confessed to being a neo-Nazi.
He wept incoherently at his arraignment.
An aspiring dictator in a major democracy tweeted all night
about communists, detention camps, and mass deportations.

He vows carnage for his political enemies.

It is precisely 7am.
A police siren howls in the distance.
Bleeding through the shutters,
the sun has already scaled the horizon.
My heart's pounding feet are racing to catch up.

To a Mother in Gaza

Late in the day,
your lips press the forehead of your infant.
You give your breast to quell the howling
hunger or colic,

the crying that babies do at that hour,
when on ordinary afternoons
you're preparing *rummaniyeh* for supper.

But rockets are falling on the rooftops.
They've been falling all day.

Where is *Sitti*? Where an older sister?
O Mother!
Bombs are exploding,
a cold rain falls,
and there is no food.

III.

Nothingness is no thing at all.

Before it became clear that I had no wherewithal in math or physics, I fancied becoming an astronomer. For my ninth birthday, my parents presented me with a little telescope. It quickly became my prized possession. I loved being out under the stars of deep night. I memorized all the constellations and I knew all their stories from Greek mythology. But one December night, in the backyard brimming with the exhalations of jasmine and citrus blossom, I gazed at the crescent moon hovering in an orb of cobalt blue air. I knew that it wasn't the science I was after, but the convergence of sight, smell, touch, the warm air on my skin, the rising dew--the pure poetic beauty of all that existed. The world seemed to me so ancient and so new, to appropriate a phrase I learned later from Augustine. I knew that I was in this world, a part of it. I wouldn't have known anything about the "veil of Maya," but I sensed that the science I craved was somehow cold and disembodied; and that on the other hand, I needed to be in the warmer house of the arts. I knew that back then, when I was little.

              Journal entry

In the penumbra of adolescence
      (and the mind's growing amplitude)

when on a Sunday morning
prone on the living room rug,
head propped on your elbows,
you read at your mother's slippered feet
the book you'd asked for
and received for your birthday

about the solar system, how it was birthed
from an explosion of an invisible kernel in the void,
and stars and planets spiraled out cosmic froth.

Your own body, too, with all of earth's bodies,
riding the waves in a star-flecked sluice of Milky Way.

The beauty of the world! The paragon of animals!
You will memorize these words that await you
in ninth grade English class, a few years from today.

Cut just now to your mother on the couch
paging through *The Times*, sipping her second
morning coffee—

When you were an infant
and for the first time recognized your face
and patted your own hand in a mirror,
your mother cooed.

At four, when you understood a world
lay under your feet and you made your toy shovel enter it,
she said, *Dig deep! Dig all the way to China!*

Now in the expanding galaxy of your mind
you say, *I'm a child, yes. But I'm becoming something more—*

You mother folds the newspaper lengthwise
You watch her lower it to her lap,
as she rests the coffee cup on the side table.
And you're sitting up studying this. Waiting.

Appalachian Morning

Six o'clock.

Not yet warm enough for thermals to lift
red-shouldered hawks and golden eagles
into their high-altitude gyres.

But the sky is flowering into dawn,
and the sun's fingers flash pink and gold.

Coasting along the side of a mountain,
I come to a shallow curve and a wide gravel shoulder
at the edge of a sheer drop to a valley floor.
Semis and SUVs thrum and whine past me.
I steer into the quiet and stop.

It's just me now, and the sun
bellying up to the horizon,
sliding its long legs over the sill of the world,
planting its feet on the cool carpet of aquamarine air,
splaying its toes among the houses and trees.

Streetlights of the little towns blink out,
one by one.

What the Venerable Bede Told
   (a Variation on the Text, in Eleven Statements)

A bitterly cold night when the king's man sits down to dinner.

He nods to the others at table,
but his mind is on the suckling pig and roasted fowl
glistening in the firelight.

He's not hungry so much as pensive
about his worn body and the creatures on his plate
that for the sake of *his* life were separated from *theirs*.

He considers their masticated parts
advancing through the muscular coil
of his gut with its acids and contractions.

Essences will distill into humors.
What is irreducible will pass into the earth.
His own flesh will be no different.

Why this dissolution into quotidian dust?
The man is tired, and the old gods don't console.

A sparrow suddenly blunders into the hall,
beating its wings over the blazing tapers.

It dives and wheels frantically before finding a window
and fleeing back into the night.

Now the man is thrown from his mood.

His mind's eye follows the bird into the blue-black
realm of stars, ice-clad trees, silvered rivers,
fish swollen with eggs hovering over
sedimentary bottoms.

What if the darkness isn't a void, but a world quietly
waiting, a womb ripening toward light?

O, Doves!
(Lima, Peru, 6 am)

"and he saw the Spirit of God descending
like a dove . . ."
                                        Matt 3:16.

Shy ones, the shades of buttermilk
and cirrus cloud,

      forgive the man and woman
cursing the scrabble of your bones on the
bedroom window ledge.

They are harried creatures
waking out of sleep's egg
      into the greasy clot of day.

They know only hunger,
      which is the world's stark treason,

and the mockery of iridescent necks
      pecking the gray flagstones for crumbs.

How can they love the immaculate
      cooing of your beaks so high in the blue air,

having forgotten the signs
              of invisible things?

Stephansplatz
(Vienna, 7pm)

At last the rains are spent.
The sky is an empty purse.
Buildings are stacks of gleaming coins.

All day I rocked and pitched
on the summer swells
flooding the humid streets.

In enameled palatial halls
I saw portraits of emperors,
and the confectioner fantasies of their wives' gowns.

But my skin was a sodden cape,
from my head to the soles of my feet.
It pressed against my shoulders and knees.

Now, in the spacious square,
the cathedral suddenly begins to throb.
It is the start of something, an abrupt arrival.

Out of the black tunnels of the metro
people are streaming, as at the resurrection
on the last day.

They flood the bakeries and kebab shops,
theaters and restaurants, kiosks selling
scarves, leather goods, and newspapers.

And the first faint stars break through.
I watch the sun's low orange wheel grind
the last gray cloud.

I turn and listen to the words the bells speak,
calling, lifting all of us like doves into the air,
holy, holy, holy natives of the earth.

House Painter, New Jersey, 1955

      for Roberto García

Ankle deep in damp leaves, I watched you
paint the house.

Cool days in late April long ago,
brown hand hunched heavy on the heel of the brush,

your flannelled arm swept up and down from the elbow
fat bristles slapping the wood, pressing pigment into the grain.

You worked as long as light held and there was
no threat of rain, singing *Maria la O—*

that opera about a girl, dead from a broken heart.
What made me cry for her?

Maybe it was for you and for *la joven* Clara,
teenaged mother who orphaned you. My *abuela*—

Could be you were imagining her when
on the porch you'd restored to pristine color,

you painted a scene of a mission church, its flagstones,
bell tower, walls filigreed with bougainvillea and jasmine.

How you worked the brushes and bright pigments,
water on vellum.

Painter of Houses! I always knew another painter
lived in you and would have grown large, if given a path.

After you left your island, memory had to suffice.
You did what was needed to survive this

rot of leaves,
this cold American light.

Light, as Seen from a Bedside

I toss under sweaty sheets of the pull-out bed. Across the cramped room, my dying father's voice, like a fledgling bird at dawn, suddenly calls my name. The city, he cries, is exploding with light. Surely I can see it. I pull myself up, slide open the glass doors of the balcony, and step into humid air.

> There's nothing but midnight, a dim outline of skyscrapers. A jetliner, its wingtips blinking, streaks beyond my hearing to an invisible horizon. Headlamps glide in tiny swarms on a highway twelve stories below. The river, smelling of rain, laps against a retaining wall. I will tell him none of this.

My father isn't a religious man. But It occurs to me, when I step inside, to ask if I should call a priest, to which he says *Yes, It's time.*

> At nine o'clock, the priest comes to my father's bedside with the book of prayers, a vial of consecrated oil, the Host in the pyx.

What to make of a life like a flame guttering in the lamp of its body? Yet in this room, there is no wailing or gnashing of teeth. For the moment, sorrow is at bay.

> Something flows from my father to me. Call it palpable light. Incandescence. A culmination that is not an ending, even after I fall back into the darkness of the living.

The Bus

Saturdays, too, when Papa
climbed the gray and white Number 4,
as he did every weekday to go to work,
hoisting himself up
two high steps to the fare box,
I knew he'd come home the same way he left—
smiling, kissing the top of my head.
He never complained.
I learned that love and the place in my mind
I called the Future lived in those goings
and comings day after day.
Later, when my old knees buckled on the stairs,
I saw him again: fare in hand, bones clacking like coins.
I cried and cried for no reason at all.

Abuela

In the dream,
my dead father speaks the same words
as when he was in the flesh.
Leaning into my ear, he says
Imagínate, hija—
the nuns at the convent school
taught your grandmother to write—
My lips part again,
as when he told me the first time
about the black-eyed girl
with a birth and death date no one remembered,
who saw visions and wrote them down.
That was before she became the too-young mother
abandoned by her impatient man
who refused the burden of a tubercular wife
and their two baby boys— *Poemas,*
my orphaned father said.
I turn to face him,
as though he were
the door to a vast room.
But then I wake,
and breath streams out of my body like a tide—
¡Abuela, abuelita!
Do you know that I see you, the poet at her desk?
Do you see me at mine, writing you back into the world?

Aftershock
    (after Stanley Kunitz)

Long after the rituals of mourning
when you buried your beloved dead,

and you'd ceased weeping for loss of them,
believing yourself beyond need and grief,

it comes upon you without warning,
a shift in the light across your retinas,

the merest movement of air.
The weight of it on your breasts,

as you lean over the kitchen sink,
rinsing the breakfast dishes.

This is the moment of your return to a fact
beyond ordinary cognition. The shock

of your solitude. And you look up, staring
through the window, across the dawn-lit field,

to the horizon of oaks and a truck on the county road
cutting a straight line to the southwest.

You have been riding along a highway
whose smooth pavement gives way abruptly

to a gravel road in obscure terrain.
How will you navigate this bereft landscape?

And now your heart begins to break and break.
You don't know how to stop its breaking.

En alta mar
(somewhere over the North Atlantic)

Earplugged and eyes
tethered to the seat-back
screen in front of me,

I settle into an Almodóvar film.
I am *descansando un poco*,
trying not to think.

But my inner ear can't help itself.
It's always whispering to my brain—
¡Oye, *muchacha! Que estamos doblando!*

Which is to say, we're turning,
banking to the southwest,
curving away from Iceland,
last refuge should we need it,
before hauling out to the high sea.

I crack open the shade,
peek at the crystalline coastline
disappearing under cobblestone clouds.
It's strictly ETOPS from here,
Reykjavik to the Canadian Maritimes.

A Cuban fisherman once told me of these waters.
Think nights, he said, in long vessels with ropey
fingers of drag nets combing the waves.
And the storms! ¡*Hija! Almost swallowed us whole!*

I look down on the sea that feeds.
Madre of All Abysses.
The Deep hulking in its den,
maw flecked with sea-spit

egging us on,
laughing,
daring us not to fall.

Sea Poem

Somewhere the sun skulks,
but you can't see it in the cast iron clouds.
It's enough for you to be on pelican watch,
and from your beach chair, scan
for freighters slow-riding the horizon.

A schoolgirl sprints past,
all stick legs and knobby knees,
high-stepping into the chop.
You watch her rock like buoy in a gale,
when suddenly she loses her grip
and disappears under a high swell.

You're on your feet now, running into the waves.
Because suddenly she's *you* long ago,
when a sand bar gave way, and the ocean
sucked you into its throat, held you down,
pitched and rolled you with its hard tongue
before it spat you out.

The child breaks through the surface.
But she's grinning, flapping her arms.
You are in awe of the girl's joy.
It's what you cannot feel,
since you never learned such faith,
never forgave the sea
for trying to crush your chest
with its snake jaws.
Even now, you're wondering what it's up to,
licking, probing, slithering around your knees.

Things that lift my heart and make it glad

(zuihitsu with reference to a painting by Paul Rouphail,
and after a line by Ted Kooser)

midmorning tea, mango-ginger,
        in the white stoneware mug

a black gooseneck kettle on the boil
        the thin upright plume of steam

a painting of the steaming kettle —oil on linen
        the plume's sharp bend as though from a strong breeze

a cherry tree in full bloom
        in front of my son and daughter-in-law's row house

their row house,
        its pale coral-colored brickwork and forest green trim

the blooming crown of the cherry tree
        seen through the tall double windows on the second floor

the light blue throw rug   jade vase   cerise flowers

amber the color of butterscotch
        on a leather cord my daughter-in-law wears around her neck

playing on a laptop, Sibelius' fifth symphony

how it breaks into flight in the third movement

moss   velvet   verdigris

down the block, two hawks wheeling over a weathered
          church steeple in the slant light of late afternoon

a long walk through an old city

the sun waiting at the end of a street.

Horses

for Paul Rouphail

With a pencil he draws two horses.
A black-eyed foal nuzzling the neck of its dam.

The sweep of the horses' faces,
their twitchy ears and velvet nostrils

rendered by a boy in the fourth grade
who will grow up to sell his paintings.

He smiles at his teacher. The horses,
he says, are just like his mama and him.

The teacher tells this to his mother,
and she leans into a notebook,

writes a poem about this tender son of hers
and the horses with muscles he has made

to ripple under the skin of their graphite necks.
A drawing so true, she swears

she can hear horse blood
pulsing through their veins.

In the Groove, Painting in Plein-Air

for Paul Rouphail

You got the sky's white sulk seeping down,
that far-away oak in full leaf, the slantwise
line of cottonwoods halving a nearby field.
You got the plundered bird feeder,
bee balm and bog sage jazzed up in red and blue,
that pink of the double hollyhocks cradled in their sepals.
You got the reclusive green of the Dixie wood ferns.
You got your eye and hand in lyrical sync.
Thick vellum sheets sing with color and light.
You got the shine and shimmer of things,
that silk of late sun in summer.

Crater of Popocatépetl, Jean-Baptiste Louis Gros
Artist's Statement

Hot breath
sulfur reek red
as a shark's mouth
stone teeth
magma studded

> *I was born into the French nobility. My*
> *father was Napoleon's official painter*
> *of heroic scenes. Myself? I preferred*
> *strange landscapes*

> *I was named First Secretary of*

Ochre scumble
colonial scabs on earth flesh
roads for the varicose
legs of mules and their drivers

> *the French Legation. That's when*
> *I climbed the snow-capped volcano*
> *with my friend and fellow painter*
> *Daniel Thomas Edgerton.*

Orizaba smokes
in background haze
the starved land chokes

> *I was also a photographer,*
> *one of the earliest experimenters*
> *in the new medium for*

The time is coming
¡Arriba, Popo!

> *the capture of light.*
> *You could say*
> *my approach to El Popo was cinematically telescopic*

The king's men will slide
from your vertebral back
¡O Popo, Arriba!

> *avant la letter. Fascinated*
> *by aerial perspectives, my eye— as though*
> *conveyed by balloon or helicopter*
> *hovered over the strato-volcano*

their bones
crushed in your jaw,
Volcán!

> *from the Pleistocene age. During*
> *the 1830's it belched hot ash only occasionally. I*
> *was never in any danger. I pressed*
> *this massive natural object into a small canvas.*
> *Mastered it from above, you could say. Indeed,*

You will stuff their mouths
with the emperor's flag

> *you could say I nailed it*

high on an impasto ridge.

Variations on a Theme of a Tenement
(as Viewed from the Window of a Moving Train)
With a Song Interposed

I

Melancholy in a Midwestern City

What you see from the clack-and-clattering
L train its surge and sway high over the streets
your city its belly of sandstone and iron

spooned up against the lake's south flank
factories   ruins of abattoirs
ghosts of strikers and murdered immigrants

traces of the Great Migration
one broken block following another
under the dark tarpaulin of twilight

Leashed to the horizon the train lurches west
past a tenement   solitary   austere   strange
as a spear of prairie grass in a patch of crumbled asphalt.

You fix on this vertical work
pressing into your retinas
its corniced roof shouldering the clouds.

And you hold on and on to it
sliding into the night
which closes like an eye.

II
Song of the Continent

Where once a glacier unclamped its claw
and the abyss between mountains
birthed five small seas,

Where the young earth bared its face
to scarifying gales whirled
down from the polar turning point,

Where the borealis still billow,
green curtains in the window of night,
sing

III

A Tenement at the Golden Hour

In the glow before the gloaming
the wintry almost-evening
air of the higher latitudes

stark and clear as arctic ice
you find a seat on the five-twenty
heading west out of the city

settle into sound and rhythm
the brick-and-beam tableaux
sliding backwards in the oblong window—

ramshackle rooftops, parking lots
your fellow work-weary
huddled on station platforms.

Against the slash of sky at the horizon
each half-minute more red
a lone tenement   its dark bulk.

But how the deepening sun gilds it—a gleaming
apparition. Now a prodigy in your desiring eye,
you want it to speak.

Let it be a tower, then. An obelisk.
Let it lift up your prayer
Let it proclaim *Transfiguration*
                  to the wind, the night.

IV.

*And the multiverse with its many folds of time—
why shouldn't you move it with your hand?*

Air Traffic Control, London to Mauritius

for Robert Rouphail

In my hand I hold the plastic phone
with its plasma face,

watching the app track the moth-like
silhouette of your flight and its black

contrail hurtling across the night
map of Africa.

                My son,

at 35,000 feet you've passed
Sudan and Ethiopia.

Now I've got you up to the
Somali border, looking good.

Soon the Indian Ocean will pop
open its wide blue eye,

and the sun will elbow over the equator,
nudging you awake as the stars roll west.

                It's in the mammalian script,

for a mother to follow her child's
progress through the world.

From the first moment I knew zygotic cells
were mounting their quiet project

to build your house of nerve and bone,
saw in the ultrasound the vertebral chain

vibrating with white light, saw
the little fist of your heart

pounding with the first drops of your
blood that came from Egypt and Cuba,

I knew I'd rejoice over your steps.
Your ancestors, too, from where they sit—

spirit and flesh from which
you spring and have your life.

Flashback on a Morning Walk in Early Spring

Childhood is everything
                (Shelby Stephenson, April 8, 2022)

Suddenly, shimmering in the trees, a particular light.
Something old in this bright nowness,
something known before washes over your inner eye,
the eye that remembers—

Your mother holding your infant body to her heart,
wrapping you in a blanket, laying you down in the
carriage to nap under the side yard trees.
Then you, drowsy after your mid-morning sleep,
blink into a welter of quivering oaks and beech,
drifting clouds, the sun, your mother's face..

This momentary return
of tree-glow, sky-sheen, the leaf-rush of wind.
And love's first imprint, that necessary stamp
against fear and the later hungers
that will storm the heart to make it small.

All this time you did not know or had forgotten.
But it remained with you,
though occult, quiescent,
sedimentary as a river bottom.
Until this morning's walk,
when it loosens from its bed, liquified.
And for a while you float on it,
this upwelling of long-ago light.

Imagining Wanda
or, Waiting at JFK for the Connecting Flight Home

> *after "Kazia," by Czeslaw Milosz*

Out of jet lag's murk,
out of the brain-crawl from ten
hours of ocean-crossing,
strapped into a middle seat in the
economy cabin of an aging Triple 7,
then navigating the Charybdis of passport
control, customs, and the TSA, I thread a path through
crowds and consecutive terminals to a seat at a remote gate.
Suddenly, I enter a scene I've not visited
in seventy years—

> *I am a kindergartner, blinking out of a feverish sleep*
> *in an Atlantic City hospital bed next to a window*
> *where a clear cobalt sky hints of red. Is it dawn or dusk?*
> *I have no clue. I am groggy from the medication*
> *for my severe pneumonia. At my right shoulder,*
> *a thin girl, pig-tailed, with dark skin and black eyes.*
> *She says, "Hi! I'm Wanda." She's had an operation.*
> *"But I'm strong now. Goin' home soon. Mama's gonna*
> *come for me." Wanda is ten. "I bet I can pick you up!"*
> *I smile for the first time in many days, and she scoops*
> *me into her matchstick arms and parades me around the*
> *room like a prized doll. I'm afraid she'll drop me,*
> *but she manages to return me gently to my bed.*
> *"Know what? I could be your big sister," she laughs.*
> *I laugh, too. I fall asleep again, and when I wake,*
> *Wanda is gone, her empty bed remade--*

This spotlit tableau is all I have.
I want to write a story, a triumphal one
where Wanda crossed the Edmund Pettis bridge in Selma
and marched on Washington with Martin Luther King.
Maybe she graduated from Glassboro State College.

Maybe Penn. Fifty years on, she retired from a
distinguished career as a university dean.

Maybe the story is more basic,
that after all these decades, she is still alive,
like me.

By God, Wanda would be eighty now.
My mind races at the possibility
that she could be in the world.
Even in this very airport. Why not?
She could be the woman sitting
across from me in a hard plastic seat.
That thin woman over there,
brown face ashen with age,
gnarled hands grasping the curve of a cane,
waiting, as I am, for the final flight home.

Appliance Repairman

He's not the guy I had in my head
with a name like Elmer or Wally,
flaunting a little paunch, maybe,
or even an avalanche of belly over the toolbelt.

Turns out, he's Martin. Tall and skinny,
friend of a friend.
These days, you find him by word of mouth.
Retired from Sears before they went under.
Got his own gig, now.
Works out of a 2015 GMC Sierra.
The wife keeps the books.
He tells me they've got adult children back in Milwaukee,
after I let on we moved here from Chicago.
Probably grandkids, but he doesn't say and I don't ask.

Martin's come to take a look
into my side-by-side refrigerator-freezer
that all of a sudden quit making ice.
I watch him probe with a flashlight and screwdriver.
Oh, yeah, he intones in his Great Lakes accent.
She's broke real bad, giving the icemaker
a few more gentle pokes and prods.

He speaks in the old-timey way people had
of referring to machines as though they were work animals
too old or sick to pull a plow or give milk.
As in, *That gal's on her last legs*,
by which they meant the Norge or the Kelvinator.
But Martin has the smooth authority of a board-certified
pediatrician examining my children's fire-red tonsils
back in the day.

Now I begin to fret out loud

about having to buy a new fridge.
Well, ma'am, no need to blow a coupla grand just yet!
he counsels, over his shoulder, as he walks out to the truck.
He returns with a cardboard box which he cracks open
to reveal a brand-new rectangular device he will snap
and screw into place. He lifts the apparatus carefully,
like a surgeon with a precious liver or kidney he's about
to suture into a desperate patient.

He's always been good with his hands, he tells me.
Excelled at Shop during senior high.
Not to mention trade school.
I can pretty much fix anything, he says as he transplants
the new icemaker into the freezer.
Yeah, I tell him, I got a kid like that, too.
Lives in Philly now—

Okey-dokey, he breathes, tightening the last screw
and shutting the freezer door,
She's in there real good! Run another ten years!
Sure enough, the ice maker whirrs and gurgles into life.
I write a check for parts and labor:
two-hundred-seventy-five-fifty.
And I think, Whoa! as I reach out my hand to thank him.

Asher
> *(after Robert Lowell)*

Now the eighth-decade
shadows gather and the waking
tulips mock me, stiff-kneed
as I rake winter's dregs away.

Everywhere I meet my father,
brown wool shawl rounding
his shoulders even in summer,
as his body cooled toward death.

Past seventy, I have my first
grandchild, just as my father had his.
How long had been the wait,
how short the time.

          Son of my son,
first words have not yet moved
on your tongue, yet bless the old
ones who have tended this garden.

Be kind to them, first born
and earth's newest flower.
Your name means joy,
your name means light.

Iowa Scenes

> "... *to glorify things, just because they are.*"
> Czeslaw Milosz

I.

Beginnings
(Iowa City)

This is Grant Wood country,
his painted idylls of lollipop trees
and ribbon-candy country roads.

A century on, no farmer
hulks behind a horse-drawn plow,
no housewife hangs hand-stitched
quilts on a backyard clothesline.

But wind-lashed hills and coffee-brown
fields ripple green every spring.
A blue tendril of river curls
around the University buildings,
bending southeast until it
surrenders to the Mississippi.

And the prairie flowers,
the wild bees—

I am a coastal woman from a big city.
I have a grandchild, Philly-born, just past infancy.
His parents will raise him here, in Iowa City, for a while.

From their back porch I look out,
past a border of honey locust and cedar
to a sky of fat-bellied clouds,
gravid with rain, ready to calve.

There are fates worse

than starting out in this place.
For now, it will be good.
As sure as season follows season,
it will be very good.

II.

Flyover Country
      (*Wilson's Orchard near Iowa City*)

One of earth's great beauties—
a turquoise blue morning in early summer,
the eastern hills dozing in sun-lathered air.
A father and his little son bending
over rows of strawberry bushes.
Speaking softly, cooing with praise,
he shows the child how to separate
ripe fruits from their stems, how to pluck
the sweetest without crushing them.
One by one by one by one by one—
father and son lift the fragile globes into a basket.
For this is slow and deliberate work requiring a fine hand.
High overhead, a long-haul jet streaks northwest.
The boy looks up, tugs at his father's jeans,
pointing to the jet's feathery contrail,
twin-tailed like a tree swallow's.
In that instant, from the field where they stand,
a meadowlark flings itself into the wind.

III.

Goosetown

*(what a grandchild will tell his own children
about the early years on Reno Street)*

Come evening, we lined our winter boots
along the mud room wall, like tidy children ready for bed.
Coats and car keys hung from steel hooks.
Umbrellas by their straps. Hats and gloves
filled a wicker basket on the floor.

The mud room door opened to the side-yard and the
driveway where the black Volkswagen hunkered all night,
square and squat as a sleepy bull in the Iowa snow.
Saturday mornings, we'd climb in for the ride to
the ten o'clock Story Time at the children's library.

Mama fussed over the belts and buckles until she was sure
I was safely harnessed on my padded throne.
Only then did Papa fire up the engine, and we three
rolled slowly down the driveway, braking at the sidewalk,
scanning this way and that for cars and kids on bikes.
Neighbors jogging past us toward the park
turned their heads and waved, *Hi!* when my father
pumped lightly on the horn with the heel of his hand.

Then we pushed into the street,
made a quick cut left and right,
past a goose and her three goslings
forged in steel and welded
to the top of a weather-flayed street sign,
corner of Reno and Church.

How I loved that metal mama bird!
Every time I looked up at her and her brood in tow,
I wondered, *Where are they going?*
Long necks urging forward,
one splayed foot flopped in front of the other.
I liked to pretend some important place
was waiting for them to arrive.
Just like us.

V.

Spring is thunder, lightning, rain and hail,
Damaging winds and very strong gales.
Trees topple over, tornadoes are spawned,
Soon they die out, and the storms are all gone.

"Spring," by Robert Rouphail, aged 10

Meeting for the First Time
Cairo, Egypt: 1989

When Maryam saw the toddler from America, he was standing between his American mother and Egyptian father in the entrance of the apartment on the Rue Champollion. She stopped to take in the child's perfectly proportioned face, his full lips, which she recognized as having been passed down through her father's side. The child's blonde hair and black lash-rimmed green eyes—yes, she saw the resemblance to a long-dead child of hers. The two-year-old stood looking up at his grandmother's wide skirt and stubby legs wrapped in thick socks. She bent down to lift him into her arms.

She spoke in Arabic mixed with French, incomprehensible to the little boy. As she scooped him up, settling him on her left arm, he tried to push away from her embrace. He twisted around to find the eyes of his mother, who reached out her hand to pat his back. Maryam made cooing sounds as she kissed her grandson in small, noisy pecks on his arms and legs. He turned back to his grandmother. His lower lip was shining with tears and saliva. His mother now caressed the back of his head in an effort to quell his cry and to reassure the old woman, whose youngest son was this little boy's father.

But the boy turned again, thrusting both arms toward his mother, who took him into her arms. Maryam held onto a little foot. All of this happened in her home, but she knew she was the stranger.

Journal Entry

**A Young Child Speaks of a Tornado
before dawn, Iowa City**

for Asher, three-and-a half years old

The night started flashing—
Flash! Flash! Flash!
Rain kept crashing against the window.
It woke me up.
Then the house went *Boom*!
And my bed shook. And the little lamp.
That's when the sirens began to climb into the sky.
They kept getting louder and louder.
It was like they were scared.

Papa ran into my room
and scooped me up in a blanket.
And he carried me down the basement stairs.
Mama was right behind him.

The wind wore big boots and it stomped
on top of all the houses on our street.
We stayed in the basement for a long time.
When we came out to see what happened,
all the trees looked sad.

After the Storm

Suddenly the fever broke,
the din in my head subsided,
Pain wicked away from my
ribs like rain from the roof.

In the pouch of night
the air was cool,
and from my body
stars rose
giving thanks.

The Plague Ship
(or, Catching Covid in Alaska's Inside Passage)

for Nagui

Who knows which lungs breathed
their pestilence into the air we shared,
all of us maskless in the slipstreamed wind,
laughing, lifting wine glasses in the ship's bright rooms.
We'd been vaxxed and boosted,
tested before boarding and deemed stout.

But the fever came sure enough, and the cough.
Spit thickened in our throats' narrow straits,
the silk of our palates raked deep red.
New test strips proved the microbe's hold.

Thus our evictions, one by one,
from dining room and commons.
And we who had kept clean
now kept to our cabins.

We were a walking contagion,
marked and exiled,
though for us, no clapper or bell,
no cave, cliff, or wattled hut outside city walls
as in black days beyond memory.
Only murmured pity, sidesteps giving way,
eyes askance or cast down.

And the ship surged on, gliding among glaciers,
while we in the night-sweats dreamed of whales.

What I Can Say
(having passed through the first pandemic
of the twenty-first century)

I did not die here
Not in this bedroom,
nor in a hospital intensive care unit.
They were not my final living whereabouts.
No priest was summoned
to anoint my hands and feet.
No kin sat vigil at a computer terminal,
nor did friends weep into their cell phones.
As for the liminal space between worlds,
I gave no account, for I did not enter or return from it.

What then,
for as long as there is time,
but to love the wind moving
in the backyard beech like a holy spirit.
It rickles through the screens, bathing my face.
And the sun splayed on these walls
which my own hands painted "Antique Jade,"
the white ginger jar lamps, the dresser
with the black lacquer jewelry box inlaid with abalone.
The votive candle,

and the gilt icon
my grandmother and mother passed on,
which they'd carried into every place we lived.
Before it I learned how to pray.
On days of pain and joy, I lit a flame
and sang to the Mother of God.

Ekphrasis on an Icon of the Theotokos

    (copy of *Nostra Mater de Perpetuo Succursu*
            church of St. Alphonsus Liguori, Rome)

She peers from her gilt frame,
exempt from sin, but not from the world
bristling with murder.

Perpetual Help, the name
the ages gave this woman in a painter's allegory,
red-gowned, wrapped in a star-flecked lapis mantel.

The chaste curve of her ageless face,
lips taut with worry, lidded eyes, her left palm
enthroning the little boy prophesied
to pierce her heart with a sword.

A withered leaf of a sandal dangles
from a tiny, upturned foot. The child's
sparrow fingers winter wing-to-wing
in the branches of her open hand.

Something terrifies: flanking mother and son,
a gathering of omens proffered by archangels.
The child looks over his left shoulder
at the signs of torments that await.

His mother's eyes plead with mine.
She cannot cancel his fate,
since what will happen
has something to do with a mission,
fleshy and inevitable as death.

I am captive in the gaze of this woman
who birthed and suckled,
soothed fever and flux, sang lullabies
against bad dreams—a mother who would,

like me, move heaven and earth
to save her child from the howling night.

Prayer in a Dark Season

(after Mongane Wally Serote)

Hold me in the dark season,
catch me when I fall, an ochre leaf in deepening autumn.

Cradle me in the storm,
when the hard wind harries my wheat-stalk self.

Keep me from the fire,
when my land can't breath for all the smoke and ash.

Feed me in the plague,
when locusts raid my fields and ravens bear away the husks.

Refresh me in drought,
when the river refuses to flow from the mountain.

Shelter me in exile,
hrow open your door and let me stay with you.

Help me fling a bridge across the rocks and arroyos,
let's bear toward the sea

Take my hand,
don't leave me at the side of the road without a map.

The Bread Maker's Last Testament

> *You only leave home*
> *when home won't let you stay.*
>   Warson Shire

The night I heard the clock count down
the final hours of my life,
my son-in-law came to me and said
We have no future here. This war will kill us.

What could I do,
but remind him that we make bread,
and every morning people buy it.
They'll feed it to their children, I told him,
a few hours from now, in the early dawn,
with tea and sugar—

Nevertheless, my son-in-law said, *I am taking*
your daughter and your grandson. We are going.
His face rose like a mountain in a storm,
and I became a man in mourning.

What could I do
but invite spiders to drop from the rafters,
bid weevils to eat their fill of our flour sacks?
Let bombs and the men with guns take the rest.

Later, in the little boat,
when the sea lifted its iron arm

and struck me with the cold of its flesh,
I fell into its mouth and it swallowed me,

though I was not like the one
who fled God and was eaten by a fish.
There was for me only the belly of the ocean,
and this hunger for my children more than for bread.

What could I do,
but enter it?

Resurrection in *Nueba Yol*

1.

A story in the newspaper
about the lost and the found.
About convergence
like the fusion
of African and Taino
drums.

A miracle as in resurrection,
Lazarus-like,
though without a cadaver,
or winding cloths,
or a summoning-forth messiah.

But a wonder, none the less.
And exultation in the news story
that a life had not gone down into the earth
forever.

2.

A woman in Puerto Rico,
broad-hipped, henna-haired.
And her brother in Nueba Yol,
dominoes champion of the street,
brash as a Borinquen rooster,
salsa-strutting,
shouting, jumping,
palms slapping
together, high-fiving
his victory
over his long-time posse:
Flaquito, El Payaso, and Tres Ojos.

Call it love inscribed into DNA,

despite fathers who did not claim their children
and mothers who disappeared.

Call it serendipity, synchronicity,
or karma on a Bronx street corner

that a freelance photographer and a reporter,
hearing *timbales* and a voice pouring
like *dulce de leche* out of a boom box
had to check. it. out.

They find four *viejitos*,
one with a baseball cap the color of a peacock's breast,
and they snare the wearer in the camera lens—

El Gallo, The Rooster,
whose hands are flying,
whose dominos clack like dry bones.
who's making *arroz con pollo*
of Flaquito, El Payaso, and Tres Ojos

3.

So, a distant cousin
sees the photos and the story on the web,

—*¡Ay, Dios mio!*

sees The Rooster strutting on the Bronx street corner,
—*¿Cómo? ¡No puede ser!*

and she makes a call to a woman in Hatillo,

—*Sí, chica. Es él de verdad.*

4.

Now come the business of passports
(strongly recommended in these days of terror),
plane tickets, and a weepy reunion at JFK,

— *¡Mi hermano! ¡Pensaba yo que tú estabas muerto!*

The reporter didn't say
how
brother and sister came to be separated in the first place, or
why
they hadn't searched for each other in twenty-years.

But explanations are beside the point—*¿verdad?*—when the stone rolls away from the tomb.

Notes

"What a Friend Said," see Lynn Emanuel, "The Murder Writer," in *The Nerve of It*, 2015.

"September," inspired by Henri Cole, "Casablanca Lily" in *Middle Earth* (2003).

"Five Women," this sequence of persona poems was prompted by a public discussion in 2020 of the roles of women in the Catholic Church.

"Mary Magdalene Theorizes," some of the persona's speculations about the resurrected body of Jesus reflect the imaginative, thoroughly non-theological and naturalistic ideas found, for example, on the web.

"Maker of Metaphors," tenor, vehicle, and metaphor are terms coined by the 20th-century literary critic, I.A. Richards, pertaining to the process of relating two unlike things to produce a vivid image.

"Uncle Sam Offers a Prayerful Apology," trans: *invasores*, invaders; *explotadores*, exploiters.

"Toronto Travel Notes," Abdulrazak Gurnah, Nobel Laureate in Literature (2021), was born in the Sultanate of Zanzibar in 1948, and fled his homeland during the uprising there, arriving in the UK as refugee in 1968. Zanzibar and Tanganyika were subsequently joined to become the postcolonial African-Indian Ocean nation of Tanzania. Gurnah's best known works include *Paradise* (1994) and *By the Sea* (2001).

"To a Mother in Gaza," trans: *rummaniyeh* is a lentil and eggplant stew; *Sitti* is Arabic for grandmother.

"In the Penumbra of Adolescence," "The beauty of the world, the paragon of animals," *Hamlet*, II,2.

"What the Venerable Bede Told," St. Bede the Venerable, *Historia ecclesiastica gentis Anglorum* (AD 732), chapter 13, the parable of the sparrow.

"Aftershock," the final couplet is after Stanley Kunitz, "The Testing Tree." See also the first epigraph of the present volume.

"Things that lift the heart," the line "the sun waiting at the end of a street " is indebted to Ted Kooser, "March 20," in *Winter Morning Walks* (2000).

"En alta mar," ETOPS, an acronym for Extended Range Twin Engine Operations Standards, is an international aviation safety protocol "intended to insure that in the event of a single engine failure, an aircraft will still be able to reach a diversion airport using the remaining operational engine." See Wikipedia < https://en.wikipedia.org/wiki/ETOPS >

"Iowa Scenes," Goosetown is the name of a neighborhood in Iowa City, indicated by its logo: the stamped metal geese affixed to all the street signs of that precinct.

"The Breadmaker's Last Testament," based on events in the Syrian civil war that created so many refugees beginning in 2011.

"Resurrection in *Nueba Yol*," *Nueba Yol* is the transcribed pronunciation of "New York" by many hispanophone Caribbean people. It derives from the occasional slippage of the sounds b/v and r/l in Spanish. This speech form can be heard in conversations of inhabitants of such places as Cuba, Puerto Rico, and the Dominican Republic.

Borinquen—indigenous (Taino) name for Puerto Rico.

Flaquito (Skinny), *el Payaso* (the Clown), and *Tres Ojos* (Three Eyes) are nicknames of characters in this story.

Viejitos: little old men; in this context, a term of endearment.

dulce de leche—a caramelized milk dessert.

timbales (otherwise called *pailas*) are small, shallow drums used in the complex polyrhythms of Afro-Caribbean music.

Hatillo—a city in Puerto Rico.

¡Ay, Dios mio! In English vernacular: "Oh, my God!"

¿Cómo? ¡No puede ser! In English vernacular: "What? No way [it can't be true]!"

Sí, chica. Es él de verdad. In English vernacular: "Yes, girlfriend. It's him alright!"

¡Mi hermano! ¡Pensaba yo que tú estabas muerto! In English vernacular: "My brother! All this time I thought you were dead!"

Acknowledgments (by date of publication and/or award)

"Crater of Popocatepl," NCWN Randall Jarrell Poetry competition, Honorable Mention and published in *storysouth*, 2016.

"The Bus," *Peacock Journal* (2017); also, revised, *Poetry in Plain Sight*, NCPS, 2024.

"Mary Magdalene Theorizes," *Wild Goose Poetry Review* (Fall 2017).

"Prayer in a Dark Season" originally appeared as "Sustain Me," *Peacock Journal* (2019).

"Sea Song," Old Mountain Press, 2020 *River Adventures* (2020).

"Two Variations on a Theme of A Tenement," Poet Laureate Award, *Pinesong,* NCPS, 2022. Awarded Poet Laureate Prize by NC Poet Laureate emeritus, Joseph Bathanti.

"Abuela," 2nd place, McDill Award, *Pinesong*, NCPS, 2022.

"What a Friend Said to My Face," *Willawaw Journal*, Issue 22, Spring 2022.

"As Tanks Press Toward Kyiv," *Topical Poetry*, April 10, 2022.

"Pandemic, 1918," *Pedestal Magazine*," Issues 89, 2022.

"I Buried a Little Bird Today," *Poetry in Plain Sight*, NCPS, 2022.

"To My Second Grade Teacher," Old Mountain Press, 2021.

"I Go and Ask the Trees," Old Mountain Press, 2022.

"What I'd Hoped to Say." An earlier version of this poem appeared in *Essential Voices*, West Virginia University Press, 2023.

"This small house, this big sky," *Poetry in Plain Sight*," NCPS, 2023.

"Resurrection in Nueba Yol," *Press 53, Prime Magazine*, 2023.

"The Breadmaker's Last Testament," 2023 Randall Jarrell Poetry Contest runner-up; *storysouth*, 2023.

"Mary of Nazareth" and "Marthy of Bethany," *The Power of the Feminine*, ThreshPress Midwest (January 23, 2024).

"To Jeremiah, Who Mourned the Calamitous Earth," *Topical Poetry*, July 30, 2023.

"O, Doves," and "Stephansplatz, *"Visions International*, Summer 2024.

"Housepainter, New Jersey, 1955," *Kakalak*, Fall/Winter 2024.

"Iowa Scenes": "Beginnings," Flyover Country," "Goosetown," *Willawaw Journal*, Spring, 2024.

"Asher," finalist, Randall Jarrell competition of the NCWN, 2024.

"Horses," 2nd place, adult poetry competition, NCPS 2024; *Pinesong,* 2024.

"Appliance Repairman." An earlier version appeared *Naugatuck River Review*, Fall/Summer 2024. Also, finalist, *New Letters'* Patricia Cleary Miller Prize for Poetry, 2024.

"The Origin of Poetry," "Ekphrasis on an Icon of the Theotokos," "Digressions on a '48 Ford," "Toronto Travel Notes: Carolina to Canada," and "Toronto Travel Notes: Nahkt the Weaver," *Witness: Appalachia to Hatteras* (NCPS Gilbert-Chappell Distinguished Poet Series), 2024.

"Flashback on a Morning Walk in Early Spring," *Good Old Days* (NC: Old Mountain Press), 2024.

"Appalachian Morning," finalist, *New Letters'* Patricia Cleary Miller Prize for Poetry, 2024; semifinalist, James Applewhite contest and published, *North Carolina Literary Review*, 2024.

"Ekphrasis on an Icon of the Theotokos," finalist, *New Letters'* Patricia Cleary Miller Prize for Poetry, 2024.

"The Origin of Poetry," finalist, *New Letters'* Patricia Cleary Miller Prize for Poetry, 2024.

"Things that lift my heart and make it glad," finalist, *New Letters'* Patricia Cleary Miller Prize for Poetry, 2024; semifinalist, James Applewhite contest and published, *North Carolina Literary Review*, 2024.

.

About the author

Maria Rouphail, PhD, is Senior Lecturer Emerita from North Carolina State University, where she taught courses in World Literature and where she also served as an academic adviser for the major in English. Poetry editor at *The Main Street Rag* and the North Carolina Poetry Society's Gilbert-Chappell Distinguished Poet for Central North Carolina in 2024-25, Rouphail lives in Raleigh.

www.ingramcontent.com/pod-product-compliance
Lightning Source LLC
Chambersburg PA
CBHW020940090426
42736CB00010B/1211